The Authenticity of the Book of Jonah

By

Bill Cooper

Copyright © Dr Wm R Cooper 2015

For

Dr Gene Jeffries

with

heartfelt thanks!

ISBN 978-0-9931415-3-9

About the Author

Bill Cooper is a Vice President and Trustee of the Creation Science Movement in England. He also serves as Adjunct Professor of Providential History and Apologetics on the Master Faculty at the Institute for Creation Research School of Biblical Apologetics. He is the author of After the Flood (1995); Paley's Watchmaker (1997); William Tyndale's 1526 New Testament (old spelling ed. British Library. 2000); The Wycliffe New Testament of 1388 (British Library. 2002); The Authenticity of the Book of Genesis (CSM. 2012); The Authenticity of the Book of Daniel (2012); The Authenticity of the Book of Jonah (2012); The Authenticity of the Book of Esther (2012); The Chronicle of the Early Britons (2012); Old Light on the Roman Church (2012); The Authenticity of the New Testament Part 1: The Gospels (2013); The Authenticity of the New Testament Part 2: Acts, The Epistles and Revelation (2013); The Authenticity of the Book of Joshua (2015); The Authenticity of the Book of Judges (2015). He has also authored numerous technical articles on Creationism, Palaeoanthropology, Bible Apologetics, the Reformation and the History of the English Bible. Graduating with Honours at Kingston University (England), he went on to obtain both his PhD and ThD from Emmanuel College of Christian Studies (Springdale, Arkansas). He lives in England, is married to Eileen (for more than 40 years now), has two daughters, numerous foster children, four fine grandsons, and a granddaughter.

Cover illustration
Text composition and cover designs by K. Tuck. The line drawing on the front cover is a representation of the carving honouring Jonah in the palace of Tiglath-pileser III at Nimrud (Calah).

Acknowledgements

My heartiest thanks must go to Dr James J Scofield Johnson, Chief Academic Officer of the Institute for Creation Research School of Biblical Apologetics, my tutor and mentor in so many subjects. His expertise in Hebrew and Greek is invaluable, and is always freely at my disposal. My thanks too must go to Dr Gene Jeffries of Liberty University, to whom this book is dedicated and whose past kindnesses, under the Lord, have made so much possible; to my good friend Dr Johnny Sanders who repeatedly read through the manuscript; to Dr Jimmy Draper for likewise reading through the manuscript; to Seth Trotman and Brian Thomas of ICR's School of Biblical Apologetics for their constant and inspiring encouragement; and not least to Lady Penny Money-Coutts for her further invaluable insights and observations. Thank you all.

Contents

Introduction

Chapter One: The Early Writing of the Book of Jonah

Chapter Two: Joppa and the Ship of Tarshish

Chapter Three: The Monsters of the Mediterranean Sea

Chapter Four: A Downward Spiral

Chapter Five: Just how big was Nineveh?

Chapter Six: Who was the 'King of Nineveh'?

Chapter Seven: The Coming of Yanush

Chapter Eight: The Hill of Jonah

Chapter Nine: Assyria's Revival – and Israel

Chapter Ten: The Fall of the House of Asshur

Epilogue

Appendix 1: Jonah, a Ship of Tarshish, and a Ketos

Appendix 2: The Assyrian Yanush

Bibliography

Introduction

Let us begin by saying what this present study is not. It is not an appreciation of the Book of Jonah as a parable, an allegory, a moral tale or any such thing. Jonah is none of these things. It lacks all the hallmarks of a parable, and though profound spiritual truths and lessons are indeed to be learned from it, we miss the entire point of the Book if we assume that it is nothing more than that. The Book of Jonah is emphatically an *historical* account. It is written from a firmly historical standpoint; it speaks of firmly historical places, matters, events and personages; and what is more, its historical statements can be verified. They are verifiable from, among other things, both the archaeological and written records of Assyria. That surely cannot be said for any parable.

The Book of Jonah has only been viewed as a work of fiction since the coming of the so-called 'higher critics' of Germany in the 19th century. These scholars had an unnatural aversion to anything which smacks of God's personal interest and intervention in the affairs of men, and especially toward anything which smacks of the miraculous. Therefore they poured open scorn upon the Book of Jonah. At best it is a parable, and at worst it is a lie, and is hence held to be unworthy of any serious consideration. How wrong they were.

Amongst the stranger things concerning the Book of Jonah is the fact that the vast majority of the world's population have never read it, and yet the vast majority of the world's population are familiar with it under the heading, Jonah and the Whale. They may not know the full story, of course, but they do know that much, that Jonah was swallowed by a 'whale'. Children's books abound the world over which tell the story, usually with colourful cartoon-like illustrations, and those children are allowed to grow into adults convinced that Jonah is nothing more than the fairy tale which mummy used to read to them at bedtime. Little wonder that the 'higher critics' have been so successful in convincing the world that Jonah is nothing but fiction – that, and by systematically hiding or ignoring the abundant evidence for the true historicity of the Book.

Here we shall hide no evidence. Indeed, what evidence there is shall be examined in the full light of day and we shall let that evidence alone speak for Jonah. In an age in which mankind is loath to believe anything except he first see a sign, nothing less will do.

Bill Cooper

Chapter One: The Early Writing of the Book of Jonah

In 1903, Friedrich Delitzsch - held in his day to be an outstanding Bible scholar - declaimed to his readers that the Book of Jonah is so preposterously unhistorical that, were we to believe a word of it, we should be sinning against the reason that God has given us.[1] By extrapolation, of course, he is saying that we should sin against God Himself if we believed it. It was an extraordinary, even a thoroughly *silly* thing to say. The Book of Jonah is part and parcel of the Word of God, and how we can sin against Him by believing it is beyond me. Our Lord Himself bore testimony to its truth when He cited Jonah as a foreshadowing of Himself, and nothing in Heaven or on Earth can receive a higher endorsement than that. Besides, there remains the archaeological record to consider, a record which Delitzsch and his colleagues have pointedly ignored.

Delitzsch, of course, was merely bringing to a head all that his colleagues had said before him. He was a member of the German school of 'Higher Criticism,' for whom barely a word of the Scriptures is not a forgery or fiction. They say - though on what grounds they often forget to mention - that Jonah was late in its composition, being born of someone's pen between the years 300-200 BC.[2] They cite as proof of this the 'Aramaisms' which are found in the Book of Jonah, forgetting to mention, of course, that these Aramaic words and phrases, such as they are, date not from the 4th-3rd centuries BC, but as far back as 1500 BC.[3] In other words, the Aramaic content of Jonah speaks powerfully for its antiquity, and not its novelty, a fact which stands in direct opposition to what the critics would have us believe.

Moreover, the Aramaisms found in the Book of Jonah, belong dialectically to the Northern Kingdom of Israel of the 8th century BC, the very time and place in which Jonah flourished at the height of his ministry.[4] How do the critics answer this? They don't. They simply ignore it. It is as if the fact does not exist.

In truth, the Book of Jonah does not belong to the 4th or 3rd centuries BC. It belongs firmly to that century in which its events take place, the 8th century BC. Apart from the archaeology which we will be considering in due course, the Book of Jonah is mentioned indirectly by Yeshua ben Sirach, the author of the apocryphal Book of Ecclesiasticus. In 49:10 of that book, Sirach prays, "May the bones of the twelve prophets..." – the twelve prophets referring to the Twelve Minor Prophets of the Old Testament Canon, of which Jonah was one. Ben Sirach wrote his book originally in Hebrew,[5] and it was later translated into

Greek and incorporated into the Septuagint corpus in ca 180 BC. Had the Book of Jonah been written only a little while before Ben Sirach wrote his prayer, Ben Sirach would have been able to write of the bones belonging to only *eleven* minor prophets, not twelve. The Book of Jonah would by then have been so late in its writing that it would never have been included in the Hebrew Canon, for by that time, the Old Testament Canon was firmly closed.

The same thing applies exactly for the mention of Jonah in the Greek version of the apocryphal Book of Tobit.[6] But for a clinching witness to the existence and antiquity of the man Jonah, we can have no better witness than 2 Kings 14:25 – "He [King Jeroboam II of Israel] restored the coast of Israel from the entering of Hamath unto the sea of the plain, according to the word of the LORD God of Israel, which He spake by the hand of His servant Jonah, the son of Amittai, the prophet, which was of Gath-hepher."

King Jeroboam II of Israel ruled for 41 years, from 789-748 BC, which places Jonah very firmly into the early half of the 8th century BC. We shall see that the political and religious background and setting of the Book of Jonah also belong to that century as to no other, showing that the Book of Jonah is utterly authentic in what it records. There are background details here which no later forger could have invented, thought of, or even guessed at. Nor could he even have been aware of them in any meaningful sense. Whoever wrote the Book of Jonah - and I happen to believe that Jonah himself did that – knew exactly what he was talking about, and he knew because he was there at the time.

Talking of being there at the time, there is one item of authenticating evidence which the critics hold up for special ridicule, and that is Jonah's mention of the 'king of Nineveh' (Jonah 3:6). They tell their readers that there never was a 'king of Nineveh,' and only a late forger who lived several centuries after Assyria had disappeared would have made such an infantile blunder. He should have written 'king of Assyria.' But actually, the phrase 'king of Nineveh' is no blunder, but an authenticating item of evidence for the early writing of Jonah that could not be better, for it places him exactly in Nineveh and *exactly* in the middle of the 8th century BC. Let me explain.

The word translated into English as 'king' in this place, is the Hebrew word *melek*, which, interestingly, doesn't necessarily mean 'king' in our western sense of the word. It also means a 'ruling noble', a 'governor', or even 'mayor' of a city, and this exactly reflects the state of affairs in Nineveh in the early half to the middle of the 8th century BC. At that time, all Assyrian cities were assigned nobles to rule over them, and these often ruled the cities as petty kings, their inscriptions boasting of their attainments with never so much as a passing reference to the ruling king of Assyria who put them there.[7] The cities of Assyria during much of the 8th century BC were therefore autonomies. That's what led to the devastating civil-wars that were destroying the Assyrian Empire at the time Jonah arrived at Nineveh (which we shall hear more about later).

Nineveh was not to be made the royal capital of Assyria until some 50 years after the prophet Jonah was there. But even so, was it so strange a practice among the Hebrews to call a king after his capital city rather than after the land that he ruled? Hardly. 1 Kings 21:1 reveals the practice perfectly when it describes Naboth's vineyard as being: "...hard by the palace of Ahab, king of Samaria," Samaria being merely Ahab's capital. His kingdom was that of Northern Israel. Likewise, 2 Chronicles 24:23 speaks of the "king of Damascus," Damascus being the capital of the Kingdom of Syria.

But even more significantly, the Assyrians themselves were in the habit of calling kings after their capital city rather than after the lands that they ruled. Where the prophets of the Old Testament refer to Ahab, Jehu, Menahem and so on as the kings of Israel, the Assyrian records refer to them as the kings of the city of Samaria. As a further example, Pharaoh Necho is called king of Egypt in both Egyptian documents and in the Old Testament, whereas to the Assyrians, he was king of Memphis, his chief city.[8] The Assyrians and Babylonians refer, in other instances, to Hammurabi and others as kings of Babylon, so Jonah's usage of *melek nineveh* is entirely in keeping with the practices of that time, age and place.

So, whether 'king' (in our sense of the word) or 'ruling noble', or even 'mayor' was intended, Jonah writes true when he writes of *melek nineveh*. As we have seen, it was entirely in keeping with Assyrian usage at that time. But, and this is worth noting, it would *not* have been true at any other time before or after the first half of the 8th century BC. What is so strange here is how the critics, *knowing* these things, never seem to get around to mentioning that fact.

One thing they do mention – a lot – is their ill-founded notion that it is the very words of the Book of Jonah which betray its late origin. Their commentaries never fail to mention this 'fact'. Yet, in truth, what does a study of the words of Jonah reveal? Well, someone much cleverer than I has worked it out, and he tells us this:

"Of the 122 nouns, all but eleven occur in writings antedating 700 B.C., and of these eleven, three are *hapax legomena,* three are in Ezekiel, two in Assyrian, two are found in the early literature but are used in a special sense by Jonah, and the last occurs in 2 Sam. 22 :5. Of the 43 particles, all are found in the literature placed by the critics before 700 B.C. Without counting pronouns, Jonah used 85 verbs, 122 nouns, and 43 particles. For one hundred and fifty years the critics have been searching this vocabulary for evidence of a late date. Up to the present, they have found at most, five nouns, two particles, and nine verbs, which are either peculiar to Jonah, or used by him in a sense different from that found elsewhere in the Old Testament."[9]

A *'hapax legomena'* is a word or phrase that is found only once in the surviving records of any given language, but the mention here of Assyrian is interesting. As an aside, critics have often suggested that the Assyrians would not have understood Jonah when he spoke to them, and it is most improbable that he himself, hailing from a tiny village in the north of Israel, would have been fluent in the Assyrian tongue. However, this is simply not true. Hebrew and Aramaic (the language of the Assyrian empire) were cognate languages, and a Hebrew like Jonah would have had little difficulty in making himself understood by an Assyrian. Moreover, in the Middle East of today, people – even the poorest among them - are still commonly conversant in more than one language, just as they were back then:. "Then Rabshakeh [an Assyrian] stood, and cried with a loud voice in the Jews' language..." (Isaiah 36:13). He was able to do this because Hebrew and Aramaic are so close to each other.

The one thing that seems to have narrowed people's vision concerning the Book of Jonah is the nigh universal knowledge of his being swallowed by a great sea-creature. Even conservative scholars seem to baulk at the fact and write of it with an embarrassment which is painfully all too apparent. Liberal scholars and critics, of course, have a field day, forgetting to mention to their readers, though, that the Assyrian inscriptions also speak of such monsters in the years preceding and following those of the prophet Jonah. As we shall see in our third chapter, one of their kings even hunted down and killed one of them.[10] So even this, the most ridiculed part of Jonah's book, belongs firmly to the 8th century BC when the Assyrians of that time were themselves writing of sea monsters, and not to the 4th or 3rd centuries BC when they weren't. In fact, they weren't writing anything after 612 BC, because in that year the city of Nineveh was destroyed.

Footnotes to Chapter One

1. Delitzsch, *Babel and Bible*, p. 88.
2. *Peake's Commentary* (1919), p. 556.
3. See Woods, '*Introduction to the Book of Jonah*', p. 2. The Aramaisms number just five in the Book of Jonah (see Aalders, p. 9). We shall encounter and discuss one or two of them as we proceed.
4. Ibid: "However, these Aramaisms appear in early as well as late Old Testament books, appear in ancient Near Eastern texts as early as 1500 B.C., and were more prevalent in the Galilean region where Jonah was from."
5. *Interpreters Dictionary of the Bible*, vol 1, p. 509. Ben Sirach's is the earliest mention of Jonah [counted among the twelve prophets] outside the Bible.
6. Tobit 14:4 – "I trust God's Word that Jonah spoke about Nineveh..." (CEB)
7. Woods, '*Introduction to the Book of Jonah*', p. 6.
8. Wilson, '*Authenticity of Jonah*, part 2, p. 453.
9. Wilson, '*Authenticity of Jonah*, part 1, p. 297.
10. The king concerned was Tiglath-pileser I (ca 1100 BC); see Wiseman, p. 6, and Chapter Three below.

Chapter Two: Joppa and the Ship of Tarshish

The Ship of Tarshish looms large in the Book of Jonah, and is a very important indicator of the Book's date and authenticity. It carries the kind of detail which a later forger would easily have got wrong. However, what Jonah gives us through seemingly insignificant and incidental details in its first chapter, is entirely authentic for the 8th century BC.

The name of Tarshish has reduced many a commentator to tears over the past century and a half. That's because of its geography. It is difficult to decide where Tarshish lies. Suggestions range from Spain and all the way round Africa to India and Sri Lanka. Even England and the New World have been bandied about as possible candidates. But, happily, the actual location of Tarshish need not concern us here. It most definitely was a place, but what concerns us is the ship that Jonah boarded to get there, and whatever archaeology can tell us about its type and construction. If it belongs to the times of which Jonah treats, then all well and good. But if not, well, that's why the subject holds such importance.

The first thing that we need to take careful note of is the fact that the phrase 'Ship of Tarshish' seems to have died out in the 6th century BC, the prophet Ezekiel seemingly being the last on record to use the phrase:

> "The ships of Tarshish did sing of thee in thy market: and thou wast replenished, and made very glorious in the midst of the seas. Thy rowers have brought thee into great waters: the east wind hath broken thee in the midst of the seas." (Ezekiel 27:25-26)

Some forger living 300 or 400 years later would not have known the phrase. But of interest to us here is when Ezekiel says, "Thy rowers have brought thee into great waters..." Rowing and the use of oars seems to have characterised the Ships of Tarshish. In Classical Greek, the very word for oar was *tarsos*, this word being the Greek cognate of the Hebrew 'Tarshish.'1 So it seems that the place Tarshish (wherever it was) gave its name in time to the type of ship which originated there, one which carried oars as well as sail. For the Greeks, at least, a Ship of Tarshish was a ship of oars. Jonah speaks true then when he tells us that the sailors on board Jonah's vessel "....rowed hard to bring it to the land..." (Jonah 1:13).

Another authenticating feature of the Book of Jonah regarding this ship is an Aramaic word that Jonah uses, *sephinah*, meaning a vessel that is roofed in or covered over with a deck (Jonah 1:5).2 It tells us that Jonah was able to go below decks where he fell asleep.[3] Jonah follows his use of the word by telling us that he "...was gone down into the sides of the ship....," and uses the word, therefore, in its correct derivative from the Hebrew root *safan*, to cover over. The detail is important, because in the very same verse - as in the two preceding verses - Jonah uses the usual Hebrew word for ship, *oniyyah*. But here, and only here, he uses *sephinah*. No forger would have thought of it.

Another word used by Jonah which is entirely authentic to the maritime setting, is *mallachim* – mariners (Jonah 1:5). It is derived directly from the Hebrew *melach*, meaning salt. Amusingly, even in modern English we still call mariners 'salts', for the fact that they sail on the salty sea. It is interesting that Jonah uses *mallachim*, because when Ezekiel talks of seafarers in general, he uses the common Hebrew word *yammim* (Ezekiel 26:17 – *yammim* being also the plural of *yam* - sea). Ezekiel, as far as we know, was never in direct contact with sailors of any description (his exile to Babylon carried him in the opposite direction to the sea). But Jonah uses the locally authentic colloquial nautical term - *mallachim*.[4]

Likewise, when we read of the captain of the vessel, Jonah calls him *rab hachobel* – master of sailors (lit. 'rope-pullers'). The title *rab* – master or captain - is a Phoenician word, the telling point here being that the ship was a Phoenician vessel, and its captain would have been addressed by his Phoenician title, *rab*.[5] Jonah knew this. A later forger wouldn't have known it.

There's something else in all this that no later forger would have thought of, and that is the name of Joppa. The port itself would have been known well enough to him. It was the only safe haven along the Phoenician coast for some fifty miles, and was hence as busy a port in the time of the Maccabees as ever it had been in more ancient times. To the Egyptians and the Assyrians, it was known as *Iapu*. To the Hebrews, from Joshua's day to that of Jonah, it was known as *Yapo* (which is how Jonah spells it). To the Phoenicians, it was *Ioppe*. It only became known as Joppa under Alexander the Great during the late 4th century BC.[6] Any forger of the Scriptures who was working after Alexander the Great's conquest of 332 BC – which is itself more than 100 years before the time when the critics say the Book of Jonah was written – would have used the spelling then current. But the Book of Jonah spells the port's name exactly as it was spelt back in the 8th century BC and even before. It's something that no forger would have thought of, and which the critics forget to explain.

In this context, it is interesting to note that, even if our Maccabaean forger had been fluent enough in Classical Hebrew to produce the Book of Jonah, it would have been unavoidably and heavily laced with Greek terms, words and spellings. Yet in all the text of Jonah, there is not a single word that betrays any Greek influence or derivation. That's because Jonah flourished and his Book was written before the Babylonian Captivity under Nebuchadnezzar in 605 BC when Greek influence suddenly burgeoned in the Middle East.[7] Had there been the slightest trace of Greek in the text of Jonah, the critics would have latched onto it immediately. Yet this is one area in which they keep a profound and deafening silence. The Book of Jonah is pure Hebrew, just as we'd expect it to be.

Footnotes to Chapter Two

1. Torr, *Ancient Ships*, p. 2. The word *tarsos* in Classical Greek also carries the suggestion of a feathered wing. The word has been replaced in modern Greek by *pteron*, also meaning both feather and oar. Interestingly, even English-speaking boatmen still speak today of 'feathering' the oars. It seems that the nautical world is a very conservative world.

2. Young's Analytical Concordance, p. 880.

3. Aalders, p. 9, citing Wilson's, '*The Authenticity of Jonah*'. Princeton Theological Review, vol. XVI, p. 443.

4. Redford, p. 54.

5. Rab - meaning 'chief' - appears throughout the Old Testament, but in the Book of Jonah it is used in its Aramaic/Phoenician nautical setting.

6. *Interpreter's Dictionary of the Bible*, vol. 2, p. 971.

7. See my *Authenticity of the Book of Daniel*, chapter 1.

Chapter Three: The Monsters of the Mediterranean Sea

"Now the LORD had prepared a great fish to swallow up Jonah...." (Jonah 1:17)

Archaeology is a wonderful thing, but it surely cannot tell us anything about the great fish that swallowed Jonah, can it? Well, actually, yes, yes it can. Or at least it can tell us this much. We are very used to hearing the scorn that is poured these days upon the story of 'Jonah and the Whale'. But what we are not used to seeing is the considerable amount of archaeological and written evidence which suggests most strongly that the story is by no means a matter for scorn. For some reason, this evidence is kept from us by the critics, or at best it is played down. Therefore, we shall consider such evidence as there is in this chapter and see for ourselves whether it renders the Book of Jonah unbelievable or not.

It would seem that, in pre-Roman days, the people who lived around the shores of the Mediterranean Sea were no strangers to sea-monsters. In particular, those who lived along what was known as the Phoenician shore - where the port of Joppa still stands[1] - were somewhat used to having sea monsters wash up onto their beaches. In fact, the people of Joppa – the very port of departure from which Jonah attempted to flee from God – actually kept the gigantic bones of one such creature on public display. The Elder Pliny tells us about it, and even records its dimensions and what became of it:

> "The bones of this monster, to which Andromeda was said to have been exposed, were brought by Marcus Scaurus from Joppa in Judaea during his aedileship and shown at Rome among the rest of the amazing items displayed. The monster was over forty feet long, and the height of its ribs was greater than that of Indian elephants, while its spine was 1½ feet thick."[2]

We may well ask, how historical is Pliny's account? Was he just spinning a yarn? Well, we are fortunate here in that we can put his account to the test. To begin with, was there really such a person as this Marcus Scaurus; did he ever serve as aedile in the province of Judaea; and, finally, when did he live? The answers to which questions are as follows:

Not to be confused with his more famous father of the same name, Marcus Aemilius Scaurus was indeed sent into Judaea to serve as aedile. This was under Pompey in 64 BC.[3] The rest of his career does not concern us (he was still flourishing as Governor of Sardinia in 55 BC, and went on to meet a sticky end), but the importance of these details is this. Pliny the Elder completed his *Natural History* in AD 77.[4] A colossal work, it ran to 37 books. His account of the bones at Joppa, however, appears in Book 9, this having been written a considerable number of years *before* AD 77; which means that the public display of the monster's bones would still have been fresh in the public memory. Indeed, there would have been those still living who could remember seeing the bones as children, and Pliny would surely not have risked public ridicule as a liar by making up false and silly stories – not when there were so many witnesses around to challenge him. Besides, he was accurate enough when he wrote of Marcus Scaurus, so why should he not be accurate when he mentions – and describes in detail – the monster's bones?

Now, any critic worth his salt will tell us right speedily that the bones must have been those of a whale. But is that feasible? Hardly. The people living along the shores of the Mediterranean depended on the local sea-life for their health and wellbeing. They still do, in fact. Their smacks fished the waters on a daily basis (often twice daily), and they would have known only too well what a whale looked like. There were (and are) at least five species of whale belonging to the Mediterranean, and the locals would have been familiar with all of them. After all, a whale provided - in great plenty - several very useful and expensive products, all of which found their way onto the dressing tables and into the lamps of Rome. Whales washed up onto beaches were as familiar a sight back then as now, and it is impossible to imagine the citizens of Joppa – a major fishing port then as now – getting all excited over some whale bones, and certainly not so excited as to place them on public display as those of a monster. They would have become an instant laughing-stock.

That the bones of Joppa were of a special kind explains why Marcus Scaurus went to all the bother and expense of purloining them and shipping them off to Rome for public display in the Scaurus Theatre - the largest theatre Rome has ever seen – and which he had especially built for the occasion. It could seat 80,000 spectators, many of whom would have known what whale bones look like. Had any one of *them* seen him trying to pass off whale bones as those of a monster, it would have resulted in him being laughed out of the city, as a laughingstock, a proverb, and a credulous fool. Roman spectators were never noted for their kindness and forbearance, especially where the Roman nobility were concerned.

There was clearly something strange and spectacular about the skeleton which made it worthy of such display, its sheer size alone being one subject of wonder. But it raises the question, just how 'scientific' or careful were the Romans when it came to examining such finds. Being masters of weights and measures, they were this careful:

> "Turranius has stated that a monster was cast ashore on the coast at Cadiz that had 24 feet of tail-end between its two fins, and also 120 teeth, the biggest 9 inches and the smallest 6 inches long."[5]

This account appears in Pliny immediately before his report of the Joppa bones. There is a precision here which suggests most strongly that Pliny was being entirely honest. It is too concise and clipped for an invention. Forgers and inventors of fables like to embellish their work, thinking that it lends them credibility. But that is entirely absent here. Besides, there is another witness to this monster besides Pliny, and his name is Pausanias.[6]

But Pliny and Pausanias were by no means the only ancient writers to report on such phenomena. Herodotus, for one, tells us of a Persian naval expedition, under one Mardonios, which was wrecked off the shore of Mount Athos. Many of the crew would have survived but for the feeding frenzy that their presence in the water excited among the local sea monsters:

> "For the sea about Athos abounds in monsters beyond all others; and so a portion were seized and devoured by these animals...."[7]

It is interesting to see how the modernist school has dealt with this statement. Waterfield, for instance, translates Herodotus' monsters as sharks.[8] However, Herodotus does not identify the creatures as sharks. If he'd wanted to say sharks, he would have used one of the several words that the Greeks of his day used for shark – *galeos, lamia, zygaena, carcharias*, or what have you. The Greeks had different names for the different species of shark which swam in the Mediterranean. They knew a shark when they saw one. But Herodotus doesn't say that these were sharks of any description. He pointedly uses the word *therion*, monsters or 'beasts of the sea,' the very same word that John uses centuries later when he writes: "And I stood upon the sand of the sea, and saw a beast [*therion*] rise up out of the sea...." (Revelation 13:1). A *therion* was no shark.

Whatever a *therion* was, it was clearly distinguished among the Greek writers from a *ketos*, a 'dog-headed sea-dragon,'[9] and a *hippokampos*, which, as its name implies, was a 'mer-' or 'sea-horse.' We shall meet again with this 'sea-horse' very shortly, but the *ketos* – the dog-headed sea-dragon – appears in accounts from ca 700BC and all the way up to ca AD 500. Among the authors who mention it are: Claudius Aelianus in his *De Natura Animalium* (ca AD 175-235); Aristophanes (448-380 BC); Diodorus Siculus (ca 60 BC – AD 30); Euripides (ca 480-406 BC); Eustathius (ca AD 300-377); Hesychius (5th century CE); Homer (9th-8th century BC); Lychophron (285-247 BC); Manilius (1st century CE); the Phoenician grammarian, Johannes Moschus (6th century CE); Oppian of Apamea (ca AD 200); Pausanias (2nd century CE), and Marcus Terentius Varro (116-27 BC).

But surely, *ketos* means 'whale,' doesn't it? Does *ketos* not appear in the Greek Gospel of Matthew (12:40), where our Lord refers to Jonah being in the whale's belly? Well, yes it does, but the word 'whale' is a complete mistranslation of *ketos*. Young's Analytical Concordance has it exactly right when it refers to the *ketos* of Matthew 12 as a 'great seamonster.'[10] It was first translated into English (from the Latin Vulgate) as 'whale' in the 1388 Wycliffe Bible, a rendering which William Tyndale carried over into his 1526 translation of the Greek New Testament, and so it has stuck fast. But a *ketos* was not a whale. Those who first heard our Lord refer to Jonah having been inside its belly, would have known exactly what it was – a monstrous 'dog-headed sea-dragon.'[11] Appendix 1 at the end of this book contains a clear picture of one painted by early Christians.

Another sea monster known to the Mediterranean world was the *hippokampos*. Our earliest reference to it by this name is from the poet Laevius who flourished about 300 BC.[12] Its name literally translates as 'sea horse,' but you definitely couldn't have put this one in an aquarium. It was nothing like the sea horse that we know.

Pausanias describes the creature (or at least the statue of one that existed in his own day) as a 'horse like a sea-monster below the breast.'[13] He also mentions 'an enormous seamonster's skull' which was kept at a sanctuary of Asklepios, which was probably that of a *hippokampos*.[14] But here's the extraordinary thing – *hippokampoi* were not just familiar to the Greeks and Romans. The Assyrians (to whom Jonah was later to preach) have also left us an account of one which matches the descriptions of the Greek *hippokampos* exactly.

Our knowledge of this comes from an Assyrian inscription of King Tiglath-pileser I, who flourished ca 1100 BC. It was found written on a clay foundation cylinder under the ruins of the temple of Anu-Adad in the Assyrian city of Asshur, and amongst all the tiresome boasting of conquest, murder and mayhem, it says that, as the king was crossing the Mediterranean Sea in ships which he'd purloined from Arvad,: "I killed a *nahiru*, which they call 'sea horse' on the high sea."[15]

This adds considerably to our understanding of these creatures. The word *nahiru* denotes 'a blower - one who blows or breathes,' indicating that the *hippokampos* was an air-breathing sea creature, though whether mammalian or reptilian we cannot know. It must have been an impressive size for Tiglath-Pileser to boast about having killed it. But here is the curious thing. Luckenbill, on whose translation our quote is based, decided to translate *nahiru* as 'narwhal.' Where on earth that idea came from, I do not know. Tiglath-pileser specifically tells us that it was a creature that was known to others around the Mediterranean as a sea horse, a *hippokampos*, which, having a head which resembled that of a horse, looks absolutely nothing like a narwhal. Of all the creatures in the sea, nothing looks less like a horse than a narwhal does, but it is interesting to see how the modernist school deals with such inscriptions.

In his invaluable book, *Ancient Near Eastern Texts* (ANET – see Bibliography), Pritchard supplies the following references to sea-monsters as they were known to the Assyrians and Babylonians: "The monsters of the sea look upon thy light..." (p. 388); "The monsters of the sea which are full of terror..." (p.389); a "water monster" (p. 417); "...who subdued the Kusarikku [a great sea monster] in the midst of the sea." (p. 514); and the "lahama" (p. 649).[16] Boscawen adds to all this by telling us that such creatures were collectively known as *umami sa tehamte*, 'beasts of the sea.'[17]

We could say so much more.[18] But having said all of this, we must now return to the Book of Jonah to see (if we can) what it was that swallowed him and carried him down into the very depths. The Hebrew gives us simply the generic term, *dag gadol*, a 'great fish' (Jonah 1:17), *dag* being used for anything that lives in the sea. For a clearer idea of what this creature was, we may turn to

Matthew 12:40, where our Lord uses the word *ketos* for the creature. Assuming that that word had not changed its meaning by then – and we have seen that mentions of the *ketos* are to be found in authors as late as the 6th century CE – then we are entitled to conclude that it was a truly monstrous beast whose head appeared dog-like to distant observers. But unless someone finds the bones of such a creature, then we can never know if it was piscine, mammalian or reptilian. But see the painting in Appendix 1.

Exactly what the creature might have been is, however, not the information we were seeking, even though we have learned incidentally what it was. We were seeking information on what archaeology might have to say in order to determine how true to the historical record the first chapter of the Book of Jonah really is. Critics have said since Victorian times that it is not at all true to the record. What record they were consulting though is something of a mystery, for we have seen that archaeology has told us that such creatures were well known and written about in the ancient world, and that the Mediterranean Sea was their habitat. Is this the record to which the Book of Jonah is true? Yes, yes it is. But archaeology is not yet finished with the Book of Jonah. As we are about to discover, it has so much more to tell us.

Footnotes to Chapter Three

1. Known today as Jaffa, the port which gave its name to a famous strain of orange, it now forms part of the larger city of Tel Aviv.

2. Pliny the Elder, *Natural History*, p. 129. For those who love Latin, here are Pliny's original words: "Beluae cui dicebatur exposita fuisse Andromeda ossa Romae apportata ex oppido Iudaeae Ioppe ostendit inter reliqua miracula in aedilitate sua M. Scaurus longitudine pedum XL, altitudine costarum Indicos elephantos excedente, spinae crassitudine sesquipedali." Pliny, *Natural History*, 9:4:11. For those positively addicted to Latin, the entire text of his 37 books of *Natural History* may be seen online at http://penelope.uchicago.edu/thayer/e/roman/texts/pliny_the_Elder/home.html

3. <http://www.britannica.com/EBchecked/topic/526839/Marcus-Aemilius-Scaurus> From the 1911 edition of Encyclopaedia Britannica comes this: "As curule aedile in 58 [BC], Scaurus celebrated the public games on a scale of magnificence never seen before. Animals, hitherto unknown to the Romans, were exhibited in the circus, and an artificial lake (eunipus) was made for the reception of crocodiles and hippopotamuses. One of the greatest curiosities was a huge skeleton brought from Joppa, said to be that of the monster to which Andromeda had been exposed. A wooden theatre was erected for the occasion,

capable of holding 80,000 spectators." For the full article, see: http://www.1911encyclopedia.org/Marcus_Aemilius_Scaurus

4. http://www.britannica.com/EBchecked/topic/464822/Pliny-the-Elder - Pliny's scientific curiosity was his final undoing. On 24th August AD 79, he decided to examine Mount Vesuvius to see where all the smoke was coming from......

5. "Turranius prodidit expulsam beluam in Gaditano litore cuius inter duas pinnas ultimae caudae cubita sedecim fuissent, dentes eiusdem CXX, maximi dodrantium mensura, minimi semipedum." Ibid. http://www.ancientworlds.net/aw/Post/521328

6. Pausanias, p. 412. Pausanias' account of the monster at Cadiz is nowhere near as concise as that of Turranius and Pliny, but he does at least testify to its existence and the place of its death. This shows that his account is independent.

7. Herodotus, *Histories*, 6:44 (tr. George Rawlinson, p. 464). The full passage reads: 'Tis said the number of the ships destroyed was little short of three hundred; and the men who perished were more than twenty thousand. For the sea about Athos abounds in monsters (*therion*) beyond all others; and so a portion were seized and devoured by these animals, while others were dashed violently against the rocks; some, who did not know how to swim, were engulfed; and some died of the cold."

8. Waterfield, p. 367.

9. Mayor, *Palaeocryptozoology*, p. 17.

10. Young, p. 1043.

11. Mayor, *Palaeocryptozoology*, p. 17.

12. Ibid.

13. Pausanias, p. 132.

14. Ibid, p. 153.

15. Pritchard, *Ancient Near Eastern Texts*, p. 275. The quote is based on Luckenbill's translation which Pritchard supplies.

16. Ibid.

17. Boscawen, p. 58.

18. We could talk of the great bones of sea monsters that the Emperor Augustus collected for his villa on the isle of Capri. We could talk of the great 100ft monster that Posidonius writes about. A 'fallen dragon' he calls it. Its great open jaws could accommodate a man on horseback, and it had scales which were larger than a shield. Yet for all that, modernists say it was a whale, being

seemingly unaware of the obvious fact that whales don't have scales. Fish do, reptiles do, but not whales. Amazing.

Chapter Four: A Downward Spiral

The skepticism and the cynicism with which the critics greet the following episode in the Book of Jonah is astonishing. It would be astonishing even if there were no evidence in the archaeological record for what Jonah tells us. But the fact of the matter is this. There is an abundance of recorded evidence which tells us plainly that Nineveh – that the entire Assyrian Empire at this time! – was ripe for collapse. And it had all begun when Jonah was still an infant.

What we are about to consider says as much for the historical authenticity of the Book of Jonah, as does anything that we have considered so far. And it is not just the great and earth-shattering events that confirm it. Because such events were famous in the ancient world, it might be said that any later forger could have referred back to them. But no. It is the fine, close, and almost imperceptible detail contained in the Book of Jonah which is its greatest hallmark of authenticity. The Book of Jonah displays an astonishingly close knowledge of that detail, a knowledge which no forger could have possessed, nor would even have dreamt of. But first, let us briefly consider the greater detail.

The decline of the Late Assyrian Empire can be said to have entered its terminal phase with the reign of Ashur-dan III (772-754 BC). Things had been building up since the turn of the century under Adad-nirari III, but it was in the time of Ashur-dan III that they gained an unstoppable momentum. In 765 BC, there began a lethal famine which was to last six or seven years. Two years into that famine, in 763 BC and on 15th June of that year, there occurred a particularly terrifying solar eclipse which blacked out the entire Middle East. For the Assyrians, this was ominous indeed. There was no 'ooh-aah' element to such an event in those days. Eclipses held meanings back then, and they did not bode well for either the people or their king.

At least one severe earthquake is known to have added its own devastation, and then came the civil war which tore the insides out of the empire. At the same time, many of the puppet kingdoms within the empire broke out into open revolt, while kingdoms on the fringes of the empire began a series of invasions. And as if all that were not enough, there came the plague followed by economic collapse.

These disasters were felt as far away as Israel. The prophet Amos (4:10) refers to the plague of this time (765 BC), just as he refers to the eclipse: "I will cause the sun to go down at noon, and I will darken the earth in the clear day"

(Amos 8:9). The earthquake, which was of such magnitude that it devastated virtually the entire Middle East at that time, was also mentioned by Amos, when he speaks of the "...days of Jeroboam the son of Joash king of Israel, two years before the earthquake." (1:1). Zechariah also warns the people that, "Yea, ye shall flee as you fled before the earthquake in the days of Uzziah king of Judah!" (14:5). These disasters were real enough.

In short, the empire was falling apart, and there was nothing that anyone could do to stop it. If it had been a question of a lack of strong leadership, then it could easily have been resolved. Assyria had a glut of strong leaders. They were currently displaying their strengths by slaying each other. But these were events which lay well beyond any man's control, and it was only a matter of time before the Assyrian Empire vanished for good and all. And there wasn't a man – or prophet – in the Middle East who didn't know it.

Now, all of these disasters are well known to us from Assyrian records. Not one of them is disputed, and together they form the backdrop against which all the events of the Book of Jonah take place. However, the Book of Jonah mentions none of them, so where is all the close detail regarding these events that Jonah is supposed to display and which we have only just boasted of? Well, here's where it gets interesting.

We hinted just now at the terror that had gripped the Middle East at the time of the solar eclipse of 763 BC. Signs in the heavens were eagerly studied in Assyria, as elsewhere, and eclipses never did speak favourably of the future. Indeed, they were doom-laden. They were, of course, predictable events, as indeed are some disasters. Their predictability, though, did nothing to rob them of their fearfulness and foreboding. On the contrary, they became more menacing in the minds of the people as they approached than they would have been if they'd been sudden and unexpected. Fear, especially collective fear, feeds on itself and grows bigger with expectation. One has only to look back to 15 years ago when the whole world was gripped in fear as the year 2000 approached and with it the possibility of the world's computers crashing. It was called 'Y2K.' However, there being no mention of an eclipse in the Book of Jonah, how does that authenticate what Jonah tells us?

Well, it all has to do with the interpretation of disasters in general and the fears that these instilled in the people; and we have detailed information on this from the Assyrians themselves. It consists of a series of no less than 23 cuneiform tablets – discovered at Nineveh - called the *Enuma Anu Enlil*, and tablets 16-22 in the series contain instructions on what can happen and what to do in the event of a 'solar eclipse which turns day into night.'[1]

Touching the king, the prognostication following an eclipse was ominous indeed: '...the king will be deposed and killed, and a worthless fellow seize the throne;' 'the king will die. Rain from heaven will flood the land. There will be famine.'[2] Interestingly, Nineveh was the central repository for all such prognostications, whether these involved eclipses, earthquakes, floods, famines or what have you. They came to the city via ten teams of interpreters of omens, located at Calah, Ashur and Nineveh itself. But there were others too at Babylon who sent in their own interpretations to the king at Nineveh.

The king, however, had a royal answer for them all. He would appoint, during a ritual period known as *shar-puhi* (lit. interregnum), a substitute king to sit on the throne while the danger lasted, so that, should the Furies decide that the king must die, then they'd slay the chap who they found wearing the royal apparel and sitting on the throne at Nineveh whilst the real king lay hidden safely away somewhere. He would resume the throne once the body had been removed. But here's the important detail. In Jonah 3:6, we are told that: "...word came unto the king of Nineveh, and he arose from his throne, and he laid his robe from him..." Part of the *shar-puhi* ritual involved the king vacating the throne and laying his robes from him, which is exactly what Jonah tells us happened on this occasion.[3] No later Jewish forger who was not at Nineveh to witness this ritual would have known a thing about it. What Jonah is giving us here is an eyewitness account of the king behaving as any Assyrian king would.

But could not the forger of the Book of Jonah have merely copied what he saw the Israelite kings doing in times of national crisis (though in truth Israel – or rather Judea – had no kings in Maccabaean times)? The answer to which is no. An Israelite king would have rent his royal garments and put on sackcloth and ashes.[4] But he would never have laid his robes aside as an Assyrian would, for he then would have been laying aside his kingship.

Exactly the same reporting, interpreting and sending to the king at Nineveh occurred when the subject was earthquakes, and we know that a truly major earthquake occurred in the reign of Ashur-dan III. But whatever the disaster or omen, be it eclipse, earthquake, flood, or famine, the ritual for the king at Nineveh, *shar-puhi*, was the same. He would ritually vacate the throne and lay aside his royal robes, exactly as the Assyrian tablets recommend that he should, and exactly as Jonah tells us he did (Jonah 3:6). But we are not yet finished with the close detail.

Of all the things which really stick in a critic's gullet, it is the national repentance of the Assyrians at the preaching of Jonah, which each and every one of the critics categorically deny. It is alleged that such a caving-in is not only unrealistic, but would run entirely counter to the aggressive spirit of Assyria, and it would never have happened. It simply does not make any historical sense. But is that true? No, it isn't true at all, and we shall now see why.

Even before the coming of Jonah, it was the stated practice of the Assyrians to hold a period of national repentance, sometimes of one month's duration, if there was a likelihood of real danger to the empire. Traces of that practice can be seen in the following two items of correspondence between certain state officials. The first, being a letter from the king of Assyria – Adad-nirari III - to Mannu-ki-Ashshur, the governor of the city and western province of Gozan, is dated to 793 BC, and it says this:

> "Decree of the king. You and all the people, your land, your meadows will mourn and pray for three days before the god Adad and repent. You will perform the purification rites so that there may be rest (*qulū*, silence)."[5]

The second item is this. It is another royal decree, this time from Ashur-dan III, concerning national repentance after the great earthquake, and it says, "...this mourning in the month Siwan" [*simanu*] "concerns all the people of the land."[6] The importance of these details is this. The correspondence shows the intimate working relationship in these matters between the king of Assyria and his nobles (those who ran the cities), and the decree that the period of repentance should include all the people of the land, its meadows, and by implication and the very nature of the decree, even the animals.[7] And what does the decree say which is recorded in the Book of Jonah? It says this:

> "And he caused it to be proclaimed and published through Nineveh by the decree of the king and his nobles, saying, Let neither man nor beast, herd nor flock, taste any thing: let them not feed, nor drink water: But let man and beast be covered with sackcloth, and cry mightily unto God: yea, let them turn everyone from his evil way, and from the violence that is in their hands. Who can tell if God will turn

and repent, and turn away from his fierce anger, that we perish not?" (Jonah 3:7-9)

Rather than being exceptional, we can see very plainly from all this that the royally decreed period of repentance spoken of by Jonah was entirely the norm among the Assyrians. And let us remember this. The Assyrian inscriptions speak of periods of nationwide repentance, where Jonah speaks only of the repentance of Nineveh. God, it seems, required less at the Assyrians' hands than the Assyrians themselves would normally have required – and Jonah actually says less than the Assyrians would have said. Nevertheless, what Jonah does say is entirely in accord with Assyrian practice and custom in the mid-8th century BC. Nineveh was no stranger to such times of repentance. It was the Assyrian way. Once again, we see that Jonah speaks true.

Footnotes to Chapter Four

1. Wiseman, 'Jonah's Nineveh,' p. 45. Another series of tablets concerning the divine messages accompanying solar eclipses, was called the *shamash bel dinim*.

2. Ibid., p. 46.

3. Ibid., p. 46-47.

4. 2 Samuel 1:11; 1 Kings 21:27; 2 Kings 5:7; and so on.

5. E. F. Weidner, *The Inscriptions from Tell Halaf* (*AfO Beih.* 6, 1940) 13f, No. 5, cited by Wiseman, 'Jonah's Nineveh,' p. 51.

6. Ibid.

7. A similar series of tablets called *shumma alu* stipulated what was required of animals during these periods of repentance. Ibid., p. 47.

Chapter Five: Just how big was Nineveh?

It would appear from the archaeological record that Jonah also speaks true when he speaks of the size of Nineveh, saying that Nineveh "was an exceeding great city of three days journey" (Jonah 3:3). It is something which critics have made much of over the years. They still do, in fact. But they can only do that by denigrating a great body of evidence which would surely confound their theses if their readers but knew of it. Let's examine some of that evidence now.

Surprisingly, it is from the Book of Genesis that we first learn something of Nineveh's greatness in size:

"Out of that land went forth Asshur, and builded Nineveh, (and the city Rehoboth, and Calah, and Resen between Nineveh and Calah): the same is a great city." (Genesis 10:11-12) *Parentheses mine.*

'...the same is a great city' is our clue here. Genesis is not saying of Calah alone, the last named of this group, that *it* is a great city. It wasn't. But without the parentheses in place, it would be easy for the English-speaking reader to assume that it was. Rather, it is saying it of Nineveh, the prime and first-named city – the very object of this verse. In other words, Nineveh, even way back in its earliest days, was not confined to its city walls as the critics contest, but consisted of Rehoboth, Calah and Resen also, a conglomeration of smaller cities coming under the governance and geopolitical umbrella of Nineveh. From the time of which Genesis speaks, to that of Jonah, Nineveh would naturally have grown, geopolitically, demographically and geographically. So, was Jonah's description of Nineveh as an 'exceeding great city of three days journey' an exaggeration? – 'hyperbole' is the critics' favourite word here. It appears less judgmental and more scholarly. But let's see.

Halton, one of the latest to address the issue, begins his discussion of the size of Nineveh by assuming that a person can walk 20 miles in a day, and that therefore Jonah is saying that Nineveh was 60 miles in *diameter*, making it impossibly large. He then compares this straw-man figure with archaeological data which show a Nineveh that is confined to its city walls of just eight miles or so in *circumference*, which is not a satisfactory treatment of the evidence at all.[1] He precedes this by saying in so many words that if we may assume that Jonah was exaggerating here, then this will give us licence to treat similar statements elsewhere in the Bible as exaggerations also, and that we may treat them all as mere figures of speech.² Again, this is not a satisfactory treatment of the evidence, nor indeed of the Bible.

Curiously, Halton cites various early historians, Strabo (44 miles), Herodotus (60 miles), and Diodorus of Sicily (55 miles), who between them yield a mean average distance of 53 miles for the circumference of Nineveh, which, given Halton's own straw-man figure of someone walking 20 miles a day, surely yields a three-day journey to walk around the city - just as Jonah states. But because they disagree with each other as to the *precise* measurements of the city, he dismisses them all.³ Such figures spoil the thesis, after all.

It is a strange kind of justice which dismisses the testimonies of three witnesses for the defence merely because they do not agree with the case for the prosecution. Under this scheme of enquiry, Jonah is forced to plead either guilty or not innocent. In other words, Halton's approach (and he is by no means alone in what he says) is a most unsatisfactory way of dealing with the question, and it does no service at all to the Book of Jonah and what it has to tell us. Come to that, it does little service to us as students of the Scriptures. A better treatment by far is that of Wiseman, whom Halton takes pains to denigrate.⁴

Wiseman brings an air of refreshing common sense to this field, pointing out to begin with that Hebrew does not make any fine distinction between a city and the area or province that it governs. The Assyrians did. They would distinguish between the two by adding before or after the place-name the determinatives *al* or *ki*. Thus, if they were writing simply the name of the city of Nineveh, the Assyrians would write it so: $^{al}ninua$. If they meant the administrative district of Nineveh, they would write $ninua^{ki}$. And if they meant both, then it was $^{al}ninua^{ki}$.⁵ But in Hebrew, there is usually no such determinative. In Hebrew, *Nineveh* could mean any of the above. It is the context in which the name appears which tells us if the city or its administrative district (or both) was intended.

An important observation here is that made by Ferguson:

"In 705 BC when Sargon built his new capital 12 miles north of Nineveh, he indicated he built it in the territory of Nineveh, using the term *rebet URA Ninua* ('the city of Nineveh's quadrangle'). This would be about a day's walk from Nineveh to the North, while the old capital, Kalah (17 miles to the South) would also be a day's walk.

Emil Forrer, in his study of Assyrian provinces, indicates that Kalah would have been the southern boundary of the province of Nineveh."[6]

But going back to Wiseman, he goes on to tell us something very interesting indeed about the size of the population of Nineveh. Being an on-the-ground, trowel-in-hand archaeologist, Wiseman was present in April of 1951 at the dig at Calah (Kalhu), one of the cities included in Nineveh's vast urban sprawl in Genesis 10:11-12. He tells us this:

> "In April 1951 we discovered at Calah (Nimrud) a stela of king Aššur-nāsir-apli II which made a statement of the large numbers of persons he entertained at the opening of his new city, palaces and temples in 865 B.C., much as did Solomon (1 Kings 8:65-66) and Sennacherib later. He claimed a total of 69,574 persons entertained for ten days. In publishing this text six months after its discovery I wrote, 'If this (69,574) is a true census figure it compares with the figure of 120,000 given by Jonah (iv:11) as the population of Nineveh whose walls enclose an area twice that of Kalhu (biblical Calah).'"[7]

Wiseman goes on to qualify the figure of 69,574, showing how it broke down to various levels and classes of the population and visiting dignitaries from around the empire. But even so, it is interesting to see such a precise head-count. It shows at least that Ashshurnasir-apli's figure was no exaggeration. But then, why should it be? And in the light of it, why should Jonah's population figure for Nineveh of 120,000 souls be viewed as an exaggeration? It would seem that population counts were as accurate in the Assyrian empire as ever they were in that of the British. The accuracy of such counts was vital to good government, then as now. So why do the modernists insist that Jonah's figure is merely a piece of literary licence to convey an impression of size – a hyperbole? If Wiseman's inscription is anything to go by, it is accurate enough.

Footnotes to Chapter Five

1. Halton, 'How Big Was Nineveh?' *Bulletin for Biblical Research* 18.2 (2008), p. 196.

2. "Our answer to this question will not only tell us much about this particular verse, but it will also help us better formulate our sensitivity when adjudicating interpretive options as we approach other biblical texts." Ibid., p. 194. – Halton and colleagues seem to forget who the *real* Author of Scripture is. He does not lie; He does not exaggerate; and as the Creator of heaven and earth, He is not so ignorant of time and space that He would not know how long it would take a man to walk around Nineveh.

3. Ibid.

4. Wiseman, Donald J. 'Jonah's Nineveh.' *Tyndale Bulletin* 30 (1979) 29-52.

5. Ibid., p. 39.

6. Ferguson, pp, 306-307.

7. Wiseman, 'Jonah's Nineveh', p. 40.

Chapter Six: Who was the King of Nineveh?

As for the 'king of Nineveh' spoken of by Jonah, who exactly was he? We have seen that the term *melek nineveh* could apply equally to either a governor or mayor of Nineveh, as well as to a king; and that such is the elasticity of the term that the King of Assyria may be called, with equal accuracy in both Hebrew and Assyrian, the King of Nineveh. Such usage, that of associating a king with his chief city rather than the country he ruled, is again as we have seen, known from both Assyrian and Israelite records of the time. It is one of many indicators which show that the Book of Jonah belongs firmly to the 8th century BC. But again, who was the *melek nineveh* who repented at the preaching of Jonah?

The clue lies in what this *melek nineveh* did when he heard the dire warning that Jonah had brought to the city.[1] He ritually vacated the throne and laid aside his robes of office. As we have seen, the Assyrian name for this ritual was *shar-puhi*, and *shar* is the Assyrian word for king. Unlike the Hebrew *melek*, it is specific, and cannot be used for any other rank of noble or holder of high office. The Assyrians had other words for those: *hazannate* (mayor or city governor); *shakin teme* (legal administrators); *turtanu* (commander in chief), *limmu*, and so on. Only the king, the *shar*, the King of Assyria, could perform the ritual of *shar-puhi*, and it is not difficult to discover just which King of Assyria this was.

He is a king who is known to us elsewhere in the Bible as Pul.[2] He is also known to us as *Pulu* out of the Babylonian records, a discovery which was most unwelcome to the modernists and critics after they had gone to such great pains to assure everyone that the Bible was in error here, and that there never had been a king of Assyria called Pul. But there had, and his throne-name in Assyria was that of Tiglath-pileser III.[3]

Tiglath-pileser III (*Tukulti-apli-Esharra*) ruled Assyria for eighteen years, from 745-727 BC, and his rule was phenomenal. He had come up from the ranks and had been governor of Calah - *hazannate kalhu* - when he assumed the kingship of Assyria on 13th Ayaru (April-May) 745 BC. Calah, of course, was but a part of *ninuaki*, the greater administrative district of Nineveh. Hence, he was *melek nineveh* when Jonah arrived in the city. We can be certain of this for the following reasons.

Tiglath-pileser III is universally credited with founding the neo-Assyrian Empire. That doesn't look much on paper until we begin to realise the sheer magnitude of that achievement. Without a word of exaggeration, it was more than any man could ever have hoped to achieve. The speed with which it was achieved is another powerful indicator that a Hand greater than any man's was also at work here. While modern historians, conservative as well as liberal, acknowledge that it happened – what else could they do seeing it is a matter of such record? – not one of them can adequately account for it, not in normal political terms.[4] It simply defies rational explanation.

We have already seen the catalogue of disasters that beset the Assyrian Empire throughout the first half of the 8th century BC. They were not separate incidents, but were each a part of a larger and unstoppable process. Each disaster fed the one that followed, so that the effects of each were magnified. But what is often unappreciated in all this is the civil war which was ripping out the very heart of the empire whilst all the natural disasters were going on, making it impossible for any man – be his name Tiglath-pileser or no – to apply any kind of remedy or control.

Tiglath-pileser III gained the throne of Assyria through the wholesale slaughter of the ruling royal family. That alone would have exacerbated the hatred for him that his enemies in the civil war already felt. What had been the Late Assyrian Empire, was already fragmented into warring city-states, and over most of them he would have had no control whatever. The economy was virtually paralysed because of the natural disasters and the civil war, and yet, in just his first year as king, Tiglath-pileser III subdued Babylonia all the way down to the Persian Gulf in the south, and also brought the mighty kingdom of Urartu far to the north back into subjection. He moreover brought the western kingdoms back into subjection as far as the Mediterranean. How was all this possible in such a short space of time, and with an army and empire which had been, just a little while ago, fragmented and at war with itself?

The revival of Assyria was, in every sense, an overnight phenomenon. And let us remember this. There was nothing like our modern systems of communication back then. For this king's word to carry the authority that it did in each and every part of this far-flung empire required a miracle, and that is precisely what we are witnessing here. The time-scale alone for these events testifies as much. When Tiglath-pileser III usurped the throne of Assyria, the empire was in its last throes of collapse. That is why, when Jonah cried out in the heart of Nineveh, that in forty days it would be overthrown, he was taken so seriously. Most prophets are laughed to scorn when they utter such warnings. But nobody was laughing when Jonah gave his.

But Jonah's warning, and the timing of it, was not the only thing that compelled the attention of *melek niniveh* and his people. It was the manner of his coming, which we shall now consider.

Footnotes to Chapter Six

1. The Assyrians would have heard Jonah's warning in their own language in these words: "*Adi arbat ūmē ālninuaki innabak!*" Wiseman, 'Jonah's Nineveh,' p. 49.

2. Caiger, *Bible and Spade*, p. 144.

3. The critics continued, however, to claim that the Bible was in error by alluding to the following verse: "And the God of Israel stirred up the spirit of Pul king of Assyria, *and* the spirit of Tilgath-pileser king of Assyria...." (1 Chronicles 5:26). But in this verse of the KJB, the Hebrew conjunctive, *vav*, has been wrongly translated as 'and', as if Pul and Tiglath-pileser had been two separate people. However, *vav* can also be translated as 'even', or 'that is', giving us instead, "And the God of Israel stirred up the spirit of Pul king of Assyria, that is the spirit of Tilgath-pileser king of Assyria...." This multiple meaning of *vav* was not unknown to the critics, though it would have been unknown to the vast majority of their readers, a fact which they relied upon in order to deceive them and pour calumny upon the Bible. It is a time-honoured strategy which is still in use today in many quarters.

4. In the same way that evolutionists will glibly tell us that a duck changed the colour of his feathers, historians tell us with equal glibness that Tiglath-pileser III organised this reform, or instigated that procedure. But not one of them offers an adequate explanation of just *how* he managed it all. In any real terms, the overnight revival of the Assyrian Empire is inexplicable. What was achieved was simply beyond the capabilities of any man even if he'd had decades in which to achieve it. Historians are faced with the fact that what we are looking at here is nothing short of a miracle, and they don't like it. Hence it goes untreated.

Chapter Seven: The Coming of Yanush

We are about to examine one of the more extraordinary episodes in the story of Jonah. It is largely unsuspected by the reading public, and involves not just his arrival in Nineveh, but the nature of that arrival. It would have shaken the Assyrian people to the core, not least the pagan priests who had held the people in a thraldom of superstition and idolatry for hundreds of years past. More importantly, it was remembered. But first, this out of Berosus' *Babyloniaca*:

> "In the first year there appeared, from that part of the Erythraean Sea which borders upon Babylonia, an animal endowed with reason, by name Oannes, whose whole body (according to the account of Apollodorus) was that of a fish; under the fish's head he had another head, with feet also below similar to those of a man, subjoined to the fish's tail. His voice, too, and language were articulate and human; and a representation of him is preserved even to this day. This being was accustomed to pass the day among men, but took no food at that season; and he gave them an insight into letters and sciences, and arts of every kind. He taught them to construct houses, to found temples, to compile laws, and explained to them the principles of geometrical knowledge. He made them distinguish the seeds of the earth, and showed them how to collect the fruits; in short, he instructed them in everything which could tend to soften manners and humanize their lives. From that time, nothing material has been added by way of improvement to his instructions. And when the sun had set this being Oannes used to retire again into the sea, and pass the night in the deep, for he was amphibious."[1]

We know from Babylonian cylinder-seals that the Oannes myth goes way back to the post-Babel years, and until the 8th-7th centuries BC it was almost entirely a Babylonian belief. George Smith, the Assyriologist, tells us:

> "The legend of Oannes, whose name may possibly be the Accadian Hea-khan, "Hea the fish," concerned the Babylonians only, and so did not interest the Assyrians, who did not care to have it in their libraries."[2]

However, there are some indications that the Assyrians were well aware of the story, for representations of this curious being are found on a few early cylinder-seals of Assyria (see Appendix 2). The name, Oannes, is the Greek cognate of the earlier Babylonian name, Uanna, and was coined by the 4th-century BC Babylonian priest Berosus in his *Babyloniaca*, a Greek history of Babylon which he wrote for one of Alexander the Great's successors. It is, in fact, the same name as Iohannes, or John in our more modern parlance. The Assyrian form of the name was Yanush, a forename and surname still in common use today. The Arabs have it in the Koran as Yunus, but in Hebrew it is Jonah.[3]

Curious, isn't it? - yet not as curious as the following fact. Smith was right. The Assyrians didn't preserve the story of Oannes in their written mythology. Until the middle of the 8th century BC, the time when Jonah visited Nineveh, they merely - when they felt it was important - engraved scenes from it on a few of their cylinder-seals. However, it was after the mid-8th century BC that a great and highly significant change came about, for from that time until the destruction of Assyria in 612 BC, they commemorated this Yanush, or Jonah, in great monumental carvings and set them into their palace walls. Layard found some in his excavations of the 1850s, and others followed from later digs.[4]

If we knew nothing of the story of Jonah, we would have to ask ourselves why these great carvings, or bas-reliefs, of this strange creature make their sudden appearance in the palace decorations of the neo-Assyrian Empire (745-612 BC). Not known from Assyrian literature, the advent and form of this fish-man would have been impossible to explain. Why should the figure not have appeared in monumental carvings *before* the founding of the neo-Assyrian Empire? What happened that they should so suddenly appear like this?

Well, what happened was Jonah, his visit to Nineveh, and the repentance of the Ninevites at his preaching. We have seen that the King of Assyria at the time of Jonah's visit was Tiglath-pileser III, and it is no accident that he was the first of Assyria's kings to have Jonah represented in stone at the palace which he had built at Nimrud (Calah), the city where he had been *hazannate*, or governor, before making himself king.[5]

It is of further interest to note that Yanush was never worshipped as a 'god' by the Assyrians. No prayers, shrines or temples exist in which he was venerated. Nor was he yet worshipped by the earlier Babylonians. He was only ever considered to be an emissary, a messenger of the 'gods', which is precisely how Jonah presented himself when he came to Nineveh. He came bearing a message, a warning, and pointed to One higher than himself as the source of that message. But such was the impact that he had upon them that he was commemorated by the Assyrians in stone, and some of those effigies exist to this day.

It is strange how all this is kept out of the public eye, or at least out of the public awareness. What kind of education system it must be which withholds such evidence can only be wondered at. To read the critics is to be left with the indelible impression that no such evidence even exists. But we haven't yet reached the end of our enquiry. There is more evidence yet to be encountered, and we shall consider some of that in the following chapter.

Footnotes to Chapter Seven

1. Smith, George, *The Chaldean Account of Genesis*, pp. 33-34.
2. Ibid., p. 325.
3. Sura Yunus 37:139-149 of the Koran.
4. See Layard's *Nineveh and Babylon*, pp. 168, 177.
5. A line-drawing of the Nimrud monument adorns the cover of this book, and appears also in Appendix 2.

Chapter Eight: The Hill of Jonah

Tell Neby Yunus – Arabic for 'The Hill of the Prophet Jonah' – is a landmark in present-day Iraq. It rises close to today's town of Mosul (on the opposite bank of the Tigris), and has been a continual witness to the authenticity of the Book of Jonah for more than 2,600 years. Lest it be thought by some to mark the place where the closing scenes of the Book of Jonah were played out (Jonah 4:5-11), it doesn't. But, if the claims of the local Arabs are anything to go by, it does mark the place where Jonah was buried – a mosque had long covered the burial site until July 2014, when it was destroyed by extremists. Why do we say that the closing scenes of the Book of Jonah cannot have been played out on this spot? Well, the Book of Jonah is very exact in saying that Jonah sat beyond the east side of the city to watch its destruction, whereas *Tell Neby Yunus* stands at a break in the city's western wall. But that is not the real issue here.

The fact that the hill should still bear the name of Jonah at all is in itself remarkable, and is certainly worthy of consideration. It is only one amongst numerous mounds in the area, and apart from local memory, there is nothing visible to link it to the prophet Jonah at all. Only in the 1850s when Austen Layard began his excavations in the area, did the real significance of the hill come to light, and here is where it gets interesting.

You see, the location of the city of Nineveh was quickly and entirely lost to the world after the city's destruction in 612 BC. Even the locals couldn't find it:

"As for Nineveh, ferryman, it is already gone and there is not a trace

of it left now; you couldn't even say where it was."[1]

The Greeks, even those for whom the destruction of Nineveh was but a recent event, remembered the city's name and reputation of course – Phocylides, Herodotus, Plato, Socrates, Xenophon, Strabo, Diodorus, Ctesias and so on, all remembered it – but, as Lucian says, not one of them could have told you where Nineveh once stood. Strabo hadn't a clue, and he was a geographer, and Diodorus wrongly guessed that it had stood on the Euphrates instead of the Tigris. In short, the city of Nineveh had entirely disappeared from view.

Ironically, the Greeks remembered more about Nineveh than even the local Arabs did. The Arabs remembered Jonah's name, whom they called Yunus, and they remember in the Koran some of the events which surrounded Jonah - his commission, his fleeing, and even his being swallowed by the great fish. These things are all recalled. But the name of Nineveh is entirely lost to them. Nowhere does the Koran mention it, not even in that section which treats of Jonah.[2] And yet, they knew that this mound, *Tell Neby Yunus*, which stood in a sea of anonymous mounds, tells and hillocks, had something to do with the prophet Jonah. They had not a clue that Nineveh lay beneath their feet. They didn't even know its name. But they knew by dint of folk-memory that this hill was to do with Jonah, and there is only one explanation for that fact.

For the local post-destruction Arabs to have known that this hill was forever associated with the name of Jonah, the pre-destruction (612 BC) Ninevites must have named it so. It would have been known to them as *til ragimmu yanush*[3] – the Hill of the Prophet Jonah – and it must have carried this name from before 612 BC when the city of Nineveh was finally destroyed. There is no other possible explanation. Certainly, the local Arabs could have known the name of Jonah from the Koran, for the Koran contains that name. But let us remember this. For some 1300 years after the destruction of Nineveh, the local Arabs had no Koran to go by! Yet they knew the name of Jonah, and they knew that this hill – this *Tell Neby Yunus* – had something to do with him, which single fact must surely tell us more about the authenticity of the Book of Jonah than a thousand 'higher critics' ever could.

The great mound that stood hard by the Hill of Jonah and which marked the burial site of the city of Nineveh, was known to the local Arabs not as Nineveh, but as *Kouyunyik* – the Mound of Many Sheep, and this is directly the fulfilment of a Biblical prophecy uttered more than 2650 years ago. It is a name which recalls the words of the prophet Zephaniah concerning Nineveh:

> "He will stretch out His hand against the north and destroy Assyria, and will make Nineveh a desolation and dry like a wilderness – and flocks shall lie down in the midst of her...!" (Zephaniah 2:13-14)

'Flocks shall lie down in the midst of her'. That has to be one of the most fascinating fulfilments of prophecy in the Old Testament. The local Arabs had indeed never heard the name of Nineveh, but the vast mound which covered where Nineveh once stood has been known by them always and to this day as *Kouyunjik*, the Mound of Many Sheep. God had said it would be so.

Exactly how Nineveh came to be in this state of almost total oblivion is a question that we examine in Chapter Ten. Meanwhile, we must consider why Assyria was revived in the first place after she repented through the preaching of Jonah. God never does even the smallest thing for nothing, and when He does the truly spectacular – as we read in the Book of Jonah – then we can be sure that He had a very serious purpose in mind, a very serious purpose indeed - the vindication of His Word. It is something that we treat of in the following chapter.

Footnotes to Chapter Eight

1. Lucian, 2nd century Assyrian (*Inspectors* 23) cit. by Bolin, p. 112.

2. Koran - Sura 37:139-149, the *Sura Yunus*.

3. Two words for 'prophet' are known from Assyrian. The first, *ragimmu*, means a 'shouter' – one who cries out his 'prophecy' in the street. Hence our choice of it here given God's command to Jonah to 'cry against' Nineveh (Jonah 1:2). The other Assyrian word for prophet is *mahhu*, one who works himself up into a lather and a frenzy before uttering his 'message'. This is not what we read of Jonah.

Chapter Nine: Assyria's Revival - and Israel

The revival of Assyria – we should call it the *creation* of the neo-Assyrian Empire in 745 BC – is not just inexplicable in purely human terms, it is one of the greatest and clearest examples in Scripture and the ancient world of Providential History – the Hand of God – in action. Outside the miraculous and the providential, the event is of such enormity and magnitude and the timescale so small that it cannot be quantified or accounted for. This is no exaggeration. Try it yourself and see.

We have seen something already of the magnitude of the event, and it makes a fascinating study. But more pertinent still to our enquiry is its providential nature. As Jonah no doubt suspected, and as we shall see, .Assyria was not revived for nothing. Jonah was no stranger to God's Providence. Neither was he a stranger to the sins of Israel, and he knew perfectly well what was going to become of Israel if a revived Assyria were to be let loose on her. One didn't need to be a prophet to know that. But that's not the best of it.

Some 500 years or more before this event, the people of Israel were given a solemn warning, and a most peculiar warning it was too. It is recorded for us in the Book of Deuteronomy:

> "And the LORD shall scatter thee among all people, from the one end of the earth even unto the other...." (Deuteronomy 28:64)

In Deuteronomy 28, the Lord lists meticulously all the things that will be enjoyed by Israel if she remains faithful to Him, and all the things which shall befall her if she walks away from Him. It is a most sombre chapter to read. The things which shall befall her if she rebels are all likely and commonplace enough – poverty, distress, famine, and so on. But at the 64th verse we encounter the strange and unlikely warning of Israel's scattering if she should do these things and not repent. The Israelites found that hard to imagine – no nation had ever been scattered over the earth before - and it is therefore of little surprise that this warning should go unheeded. The machinery was simply not in place to make such a thing even possible, let alone likely. Nations had been destroyed, overrun, vanquished, of course. But scattered? No, none had ever been scattered over the face of the earth before, so that was a most unlikely promise.

And so it remained, until 745 BC and the accession of Tiglath-pileser III. Until his day, the Assyrian army had occupied itself with wholesale slaughter, plunder and destruction. There was no end to their ingenuity in this as their own monuments and inscriptions testify. But with the reign of this king - the very king who had repented at the preaching of Jonah - there came a new policy. Tiglath-pileser III was the first Assyrian king to devise the uprooting of rebellious nations on a large scale and their transportation to opposite ends of the empire where they were settled in foreign lands.[1]

The Assyrians must at first have thought him mad. The logistics of moving entire nations around the empire were formidable to say the least, if not insurmountable. The point of such an exercise would have been lost to them. But, under the Providential Hand of God – who, "stirred up the spirit of Pul king of Assyria, even the spirit of Tilgath-pileser king of Assyria...."[2] – it was done, and moreover it was seen to be done. Against all the rules of common sense and tried and tested policy, it also worked!

It has to be said that Israel was by no means the only nation of the Middle East to be uprooted under this king's new policy. She saw it happen to several of her neighbours first. In just his first year, the king of Assyria transplanted peoples into and out of Babylonia. He did the same thing that year to Bit Sumurzu and Bit Khamban, districts which lay to the east of Assyria. He then – still in his first year - turned his attention to the north and subdued Urartu. Then Syria in the west fell to him, and all the time those peoples of the Middle East who fell under his eye (forty-two nations in all) were uprooted from their homelands and transported into foreign lands.[3] Now, at last, the machinery was in place. The logistics had all been worked out, and Israel's scattering, as promised by God, was now not only achievable, but inevitable if she did not repent.

Tiglath-pileser III was to die in 727 BC, and still Israel hadn't been uprooted. She remained in her homeland, having played off the Assyrians and other hostile nations most cleverly in her wheeling and political dealing. She therefore thought that with the death of this king the storm had passed and that she was safe, and on that account did not repent and turn back to God. But what was it that she should repent of? Was Israel not the Chosen People – the Covenant Nation? Yes, she was, but in name only it seems.

We shall not weary ourselves with her catalogue of sins, but we shall take note of one, because this one iniquity is indicative of the appalling depths to which the children of Israel had sunk. We are not dealing here with the commonplace – thievery, adultery, false balances, lying, and so on. We are dealing with a particular horror that almost defies description. We are dealing with Israel passing her children through the fire to Molech.

This hideous ritual was the very antithesis of all that is holy, of everything to which God had called His people. It involved the Israelites giving up their children, the firstborn who were particularly sacred to God, and burning them alive in the flames of an idol. It is said that the screams of the children as they died were so loud and heartrending, that priests employed drummers to try to drown out the sound. The terror that must have gripped these poor little mites as they waited in line to be burned can scarcely be imagined. It beggars belief. No rational argument can explain why Israel had sunk to this. No excuse can be found for it. That the Phoenicians, Canaanites, Carthaginians and other lost peoples – who did *not* have the Word of God - should do such things is at least not surprising, though it has to be said that most of the unenlightened nations of the world have *never* stooped to such horrors as this. But Israel? The children of Abraham - those who were consecrated to God at their very births? That they should do such things is beyond all reason.[4] They might have repented and been spared even now. God would not have cast them away had they done so. But they refused, and nothing less than the long-promised judgment was left for them.

That promise was fulfilled in 722 BC when the people of Northern Israel were finally taken captive and uprooted from their land. After an astonishing degree of patience and pleading with them on God's part, His promise was fulfilled to the letter. There were, of course, other promises in His Word which spoke of the gathering of His people into their own land again in the latter days, and we are even now witnessing the solemn and wonderful fulfilment of those promises. But we see here, in the promised scattering of His people all those years ago, the very purposes of all that happened to the prophet Jonah. One of the reasons why people pour such scorn on the story of Jonah is that the point of it all is lost to them. Well, the point is this. God is not mocked, and is able to fulfil His promises in ways that men can scarcely believe or imagine, and the greatest driving component behind all the events of the Book of Jonah is God's Providence, His ability to rule history and the world in even the most unlikely ways toward the promised fulfilment of His Word. He never fails!

Footnotes to Chapter Nine

1. *Interpreter's Dictionary of the Bible*, vol. 1, p. 272. Some earlier experiments in the transportation of small numbers of rebellious subjects had taken place in one or two previous reigns, but nothing on this scale had ever been attempted before.

2. 1 Chronicles 5:26.

3. "42 countries and their kings... my hand conquered... and laid on them the heavy yoke of my rule." Brackman, *The Luck of Nineveh*, p. 3.

4. The prophet Micah explains for us the purpose behind Israel's burning her children in sacrifice. It wasn't in the hope of a fruitful harvest, or for rain or riches. It was in the futile hope of buying salvation from sin, for which vain and forlorn hope she committed a more grievous sin: "Shall I give my firstborn for my transgression, the fruit of my body for the sin of my soul? He hath shewed thee, O man, what is good; and what doth the LORD require of thee, but to do justly, and to love mercy, and to walk humbly with thy God? (Micah 6:7-8) – but this Israel refused to do. She would have salvation on her own terms, not His, and so she made her own doom.

Chapter Ten: The Fall of the House of Asshur

That the neo-Assyrian empire collapsed just 133 years after her creation, is a fact well documented, and the tale of that collapse is told in many history books. That is not our remit here. Our remit, rather, is to briefly consider the nature of that collapse, and how closely its events unfolded in accordance with the promises of God on the subject. God had brought about the birth of that empire for one specific purpose – the promised scattering of His people should they rebel against Him and cast Him off (Deuteronomy 28:64). It was achieved to perfection. What happened next, though, we may take as a warning from history.

We have seen that, in 745 BC, Nineveh repented of her iniquity – namely her violence (Jonah 3:8b) – and was duly spared. Then, under the very king who had repented at Jonah's preaching, a new and novel policy was formed regarding the uprooting of nations, and thus Assyria quickly became the only power on earth which had the necessary machinery in place to dismantle the Northern Kingdom of Israel and scatter her people, exactly as God had promised. Under the Providence of God, Assyria had been made fit for the purpose.

However, flaying, burning, the gouging of eyes, the torture and dismemberment of children, were still employed even under Tiglath-pileser III who had so recently and so publicly repented of such things, and it soon became evident that Assyria's old rapaciousness and bloodlust had never really left her. Her repentance had been too shallow. Moreover, we see in the later siege of Jerusalem (701 BC) that her subsequent kings laboured under a strong delusion, namely that they still held God's commission to scatter and destroy His people.

The Siege of Jerusalem is not only described three times in the Bible,[1] but in the Assyrian records as well, and it all makes fascinating reading. To cut a very long story short, Sennacherib, through his minister, the Rab-shakeh, foolishly boasted before Jerusalem:

"And am I now come up without the Lord against this land to destroy it? The Lord said unto me, Go up against this land and destroy it!" (Isaiah 36:10).

There is little doubt that Sennacherib believed his own words. But they were foolish words, words of blasphemy: "Let not thy God, in Whom thou trustest, deceive thee..." (Isaiah 37:10) – as if God Himself were the liar. Yet, in the event, not one Assyrian arrow was to be loosed against the city of Jerusalem. All that Sennacherib could boast of – and it was indeed an empty boast – was this:

> "As for Hezekiah the Judahite...like a caged bird I shut him up in Jerusalem...the terrifying splendour of my majesty overwhelmed him..." (Sennacherib's Prism).[2]

Quite so. Not a word, though, about carrying off any people from Jerusalem, and not a word about the horrifying loss of 185,000 of his own men in the course of a single night (Isaiah 37:36). The passing of the Angel of Death through the Assyrian camp that night was not unwitnessed in the Middle East (the Babylonians took the opportunity to revolt), and was indeed recalled by the Greeks through Herodotus, who mockingly wrote that the mighty Assyrians had been defeated by an army of desert mice.[3] Sennacherib himself was later murdered by his own sons in, ironically, the city of Nineveh (Isaiah 37:38), an event also described in the *Chronicle of the Reigns of Nabu-nasir and Samas-suma-ukin*:

> "On the twentieth day of the month Tebetu [Dec/Jan], Sennacherib, King of Assyria, was killed by his son in a rebellion." (Line 35)[4]

All this, though, was not the end of Assyria's backsliding, nor indeed the end of Assyria – yet. Her further decline and misfortunes are well documented, and it is at this point that another prophet enters the scene, a man named Nahum.

The Prophecies of Nahum (c. 655 BC)

Nahum describes himself as an Elkoshite, an inhabitant of Elkosh, which lay on the northern shore of the Sea of Galilee, and which was later known as Capernaum – the Village of Nahum. He names no kings in the opening verses of his book, as most of the prophets do, indicating that he lived after the removal of the Northern Kingdom of Israel in 722 BC. We may, in fact, date his book to ca. 655 BC, because he mentions the then recent destruction by the Assyrians of Thebes (which he calls by its Egyptian name of No), an event which occurred in 661 BC (Nahum 3:8). But what is remarkable about his prophecies is that, although they are uttered in what might be thought of as general terms, they enjoy a most interesting corroboration in the close detail left by pagan historians and writers on the history, not just of Nineveh's last days, but of the means and methods by which she was destroyed.

Nahum's book, a masterpiece of descriptive writing (see 3:2), is almost wholly taken up with the final destruction of Nineveh. The force of its language is startling and remarkably graphic. It is by no means a comfortable read. The whole book is on fire with God's wrath and judgment against the wicked city, affording only rare glimpses of God's provision of salvation, and indeed of the Lord Jesus Christ Himself - though such for the moment is offered only for Judah's comfort and assurance, not that of the Assyrians:

> "Behold upon the mountains the feet of Him that bringeth good tidings, that publisheth peace! O Judah, keep thy solemn feasts; perform thy vows, for the wicked shall no more pass through thee. He is utterly cut off!" (Nahum 1:15)

As for the accuracy of Nahum's prophecies concerning the death-throes of Nineveh in 612 BC, we may note the following remarkable instances. Speaking in ca 655 BC of the way in which God was to make an end of Nineveh, Nahum pronounces that:

> "But with an overrunning flood will He make an utter end of the place thereof, and darkness shall pursue His enemies." Nahum 1:8

To which we may add another of his verses:

> "The gates of the rivers shall be opened, and the palace [of Nineveh] shall be dissolved." Nahum 2:6

The truth of which is evidenced by the later Greek writer, Diodorus Siculus, who wrote in ca 45 BC:

> "There was a prophecy received from their forefathers, that Nineveh should not be taken till the river first became an enemy to the city. It happened in the third year of the siege, that the Euphrates [actually the Tigris] being swollen with continued rains, overflowed part of the city, and threw down twenty stadia of the wall. The king then imagining that the oracle was accomplished, and that the river was now manifestly become an enemy to the city, casting aside all hope of safety, and lest he should fall into the hands of the enemy, built a large funeral pyre in the palace, and having collected all his gold and silver and royal vestments, together with his concubines and eunuchs, placed himself with them in a little apartment built in the pyre; burnt them, himself, and the palace together. When the death of the king

(Sardanapalus) was announced by certain deserters, the enemy entered in by the breach which the waters had made, and took the city."[5]

The flooding of Nineveh and the breaching of her walls took place in 612 BC, and the coming to pass of Nahum's words on this is indeed remarkable. Yet there are further close details that reveal the accuracy of Nahum's prophecies concerning 'the wicked city'. Amongst them are Nahum 3:17 where the mass desertion of Assyria's army officers at this time is foretold. Babylonian and Greek records also speak of this desertion. In 3:19, Nahum prophesies that Nineveh will never recover from this disaster. Again, he is right. In 1:10 & 3:11, Nahum foretells the drunkenness of the Assyrian soldiers at this time, an event which was recalled by Diodorus Siculus nearly 600 years later:

"The Assyrian king gave much wine to his soldiers. Deserters told this to the enemy, who attacked that night."[6]

But perhaps the most remarkable – certainly the most spectacular – of Nahum's prophecies regarding Nineveh, is this:

"And the Lord hath given a commandment concerning thee, that no more of thy name be sown. Out of the house of thy gods will I cut off the graven image and the molten image. I will make thy grave, for thou art vile!" (Nahum 1:14)

God's pronouncement concerning Nineveh having a grave was no idle threat. Nor was it even an hyperbole. It was absolutely literal and was literally carried out. The fact of the matter is that very shortly after the death of this truly vast city, Nineveh disappeared entirely from view. It was, in every sense, as if she had never been. Nineveh, with her great temples, palaces, walls and other marvels, was buried over by the sand, and buried quickly too. Barely 200 years later, Xenophon tells us that the armies of Cyrus had camped on the very site of Nineveh without even realising that a city lay buried there at all. All trace of it was lost to view. Even its very name was forgotten. When the later Moslem Arabs wrote of Jonah in the Koran, they mentioned the prophet, they mentioned the great fish, but they didn't mention Nineveh. As we have seen, even its name was unknown to them.

This astonishing burial was not confined to just the city of Nineveh, but to the entire administrative district of *alninuaki*, comprising the equally impressive cities of Khorsabad, Nimrud and Karamles. Now that is a truly vast burial, and we can only guess at the might and power that God exercised to accomplish it. But accomplish it He did, in exact accord with His promise; and His promises, we may observe, never fail.

Footnotes to Chapter Ten

1. 2 Kings 18:13-19:37; 2 Chronicles 32:1-22; Isaiah 36:1-37:38.

2. The same prism also makes mention of Merodach-baladan whom critics had always scorned as fictional.

3. The loss of the Assyrian army at Jerusalem occurred at the opening of Hezekiah's fifteenth year as king, in the month Abib (March/April) 701 BC. It was a Sabbath Year (see Isaiah 37:30), which explains why the people of Jerusalem did absolutely nothing during the Siege. All present Sabbath Years are reckoned from it. The following year was Jubilee.

4. http://www.sacred-texts.com/bib/cmt/clarke/nah002.htm

5. http://100prophecies.org/page10.htm

6. http://www.aboutbibleprophecy.com/nahum_1_10.htm

Epilogue

Now, we have come to the point when we have to decide which way to go on the Book of Jonah. One of the most ridiculed books of the Bible, labelled by critics everywhere as a fantasy and a forgery, it has shown itself to be not just a feasible account, but one which is historically verifiable from that most revered of the sciences, archaeology. We have taken a journey from Joppa all the way to Nineveh, and have encountered an astonishing degree of archaeological evidence to the effect that, whoever wrote the Book of Jonah, knew *exactly* what he was talking about. Moreover, he speaks truthfully. He knows background details which no forger or story-teller could ever have guessed at, and he gets them right every time. He writes of Assyrian rituals regarding the king and national repentance that his critics appear to be unaware of. And again, he gets them right every time. Even those parts of his account that appear at first sight to be hyperbole – exaggeration for literary effect – reveal themselves on close examination to be nothing of the kind. Instead, they are accurate accounts of real historical places, events and personages. That is not something which will comfort the critic. In fact, it makes a complete fool of him.

The mockery which passes for modern scholarship in certain quarters will not cease on that account, of course. The evidence we have presented here will make absolutely no difference to the way in which the Book of Jonah is academically spat upon and laughed at. But hopefully – and this is our solemn prayer – it will make a difference to those millions on the earth who love their Bible, and who have learned to trust and believe the promises and the Word of God.

It is a matter of historical record that some 'prophets' of the ancient world went to great and alarming lengths to gain the attention of their hearers. One is on record for grabbing the attention of his city's elders by standing before them and eating an entire lamb in front of them – raw! He succeeded. In fact, he gained not just their attention, but the attention of the city's medical fraternity who no doubt had to treat the consequent bout of food poisoning. The last fraternity to give him their undivided attention were the city's undertakers.[1]

Poor Jonah's entrance onto the world stage was infinitely more spectacular than that, and yet, unlike our unwise lamb-devouring 'prophet', none of it was of his own choosing or devising. It was entirely of God's own choosing and devising. That's why it worked. Indeed, the choosing and devising of God are explicitly evident throughout the Book of Jonah. It's something that we call Providential History.

Footnote

1. Nissinen, Martti. *Prophets and Prophecy in the Ancient Near East* (SBLWAW 12; Atlanta: Society of Biblical Literature, 2003), 38–39.

Appendix 1: Jonah, a Ship of Tarshish and a Ketos

This painting adorns a wall in the Catacombs of Rome, and exhibits very plainly how accurately the Christians of the 1st century understood the story of Jonah. The picture depicts Jonah being thrown overboard from the Ship of Tarshish – notice the bank of oars – and the *ketos* rising out of the sea to swallow him. But note the appearance of the *ketos*. It is not a whale at all as Jerome states, but a dog-headed sea-dragon, just as the Greeks described it.

Appendix 2: The Assyrian Yanush

Assyrian cylinder seal impression depicting two 'Yanush'-type figures.

Line drawing of Yanush (after Layard) from the wall of Tiglath-pileser III's palace at Nimrud (Calah), the first of such images.

Although images of Yanush are to be found on certain Assyrian cylinder seals, as our first illustration shows, such images only began appearing on Assyrian monuments after the mid-8th century BC, after Jonah's visit to Nineveh. Before his time, Yanush – or Oannes – was a purely Babylonian figure, the Assyrians caring little or nothing for the written Babylonian mythology surrounding him. Yanush certainly isn't found in Assyrian mythology, at least not until the middle of the 8th century BC when he first makes an appearance on the palace walls of Tiglath-pileser III, the king who repented at the preaching of Jonah. After then (745 BC), his image appears on the palace walls of Assyrian kings until the neo-Assyrian Empire's destruction in 612 BC.

Bibliography

Aalders, G C. *The Problem of the Book of Jonah.* (1948). Theol. Students Fellowship.

Annus, Amar (ed.). *Divination and Interpretation of Signs in the Ancient World.* 2010. University of Chicago.

Anon. 'A Brief Historical Survey of the Powers of Mesopotamia.' Available online at: http://www.ibiblio.org/freebiblecommentary/pdf/EN/mesopotamian_powers.pdf

Bolin, Thomas. 'Should I not also Pity Nineveh?' *Journal for the Study of the Old Testament* 67 (1995). pp. 109-120.

Boscawen, W St Chad. *From Under the Dust of Ages.* 1886. Simpkin Marshall & Co.

Brackman, Arnold. *The Luck of Nineveh.* 1980. Eyre Methuen. London.

Caiger, Stephen. *Bible and Spade.* 1951. Oxford University Press.

Delitzsch, Friedrich. *Babel and Bible.* 1903. Open Court. Chicago.

Desprez, P S. *The Book of Jonah Illustrated by Discoveries at Nineveh.* 1857. London.

Ferguson, Paul. 'Who was the King of Nineveh in Jonah 3:6?' *Tyndale Bulletin.* 47.2 (Nov. 1996) 301-314.

Godley, A (tr.). *Herodotus: Books V-VII.* 1963. Loeb Classical Library. Harvard.

Halton, Charles. 'How Big Was Nineveh?' *Bulletin for Biblical Research* 18.2 (2008).

Interpreters Dictionary of the Bible. 5 vols. 1962. Abingdon Press.

Kidner, F D. 'The Distribution of Divine Names in Jonah.' Tyndale Bulletin 21 (1970) pp. 126-127.

Lawrence, Paul. 'Assyrian Nobles and the Book of Jonah.' *Tyndale Bulletin* 37 (1986). Pp. 121-132.

Layard, Austen. *Discoveries among the Ruins of Nineveh and Babylon.* 1853. Harper Bros.

Layard, Austen. *Nineveh and Babylon.* 1867. John Murray. London.

Mayor, Adrienne. 'Palaeocryptozoology: A Call for Collaboration Between Classicists and Cryptozoologists.' *Cryptozoology.* Vol 8 (1989). pp. 12-26.

Mayor, Adrienne. *The First Fossil Hunters.* 2000. Princeton University Press.

Merrill, Eugene H. 'The Sign of Jonah.' *Journal of the Evangelical Theological Society*. March 1980. pp. 23-30.

Morris, Henry. *The Remarkable Journey of Jonah*. 2003. Master Books.

New Bible Dictionary. 1980. Intervarsity Press. London. 3 vols.

Nissinen, Martti. *Prophets and Prophecy in the Ancient Near East* (SBLWAW 12; Atlanta: Society of Biblical Literature, 2003), 38–39.

Osborn, Henry. *Palestine Past and Present*. 1859. Trubner & Co. London.

Owen, J J. *Analytical Key to the Old Testament*. 4 vols. 1989. Baker Book House.

Pausanius. *Guide to Greece*. Vol. 1 (tr. Peter Levi 1971). Penguin.

Peddie, James. *A Practical Exposition of the Book of Jonah*. 1842. William Oliphant.

Pliny the Elder. *Natural History*. (tr, John Healy). 1991. Penguin Classics.

Postgate, J N. *The Governor's Palace Archive*. 1973. Brit. School of Archaeology in Iraq.

Pritchard, James B. *Ancient Near Eastern Texts Relating to the Old Testament*. 1969. Princeton University Press. New Jersey.

Rawlinson, George. *Herodotus: Histories*. 1996. Wordsworth Classics.

Redford, R A. *Studies in the Book of Jonah*. 1883. Hodder & Stoughton. London.

Smith, George. *Assyrian Discoveries during 1873 and 1874*. 1875. Scribner & Armstrong.

Smith, George. *The Chaldean Account of Genesis*. 1876. Samson Low. London.

Snaith, Norman. *Notes on the Hebrew Text of the Book of Jonah*. 1945. Epworth Press.

Torr, Cecil. *Ancient Ships*. 1895. Cambridge University Press.

Van der Mieroop, Marc. *A History of the Ancient Near East*. 2004. Blackwell Publishing.

Waterfield, Robin. *Herodotus: The Histories*. 1998. Oxford University Press.

Wendland, Ernst. 'Text Analysis and the Genre of Jonah – Part 1.' *Journal of the Evangelical Theological Society* 39.2 (June 1996). pp. 191-206.

Wendland, Ernst. 'Text Analysis and the Genre of Jonah – Part 2.' *Journal of the Evangelical Theological Society* 39.3 (September 1996). pp. 373-395.

Wigram, George. *Englishman's Hebrew Concordance of the Old Testament* (1874). 2003. Hendrickson Publishers.

Wilson, Ambrose John. 'The Sign of the Prophet Jonah and its Modern Confirmations.' *The Princeton Theological Review*, 1927. pp. 630-642.

Wilson, R D. 'The Authenticity of Jonah – Article I.' *Princeton Theological Review*. 16.2 (1918). pp. 280-298.

Wilson, R D. 'The Authenticity of Jonah – Article II.' *Princeton Theological Review*. 16.3 (1918). pp. 430-456.

Wiseman, Donald J. "Law and Order in Old Testament Times," *Vox Evangelica* 8 (1973): pp. 5-21.

Wiseman, Donald J. 'Jonah's Nineveh.' *Tyndale Bulletin* 30 (1979) 29-52.

Woods, Andy. *Introduction to the Book of Jonah*. 2007. Posted online at: http://www.spiritandtruth.org/teaching/introduction_to_the_books_of_the_bible/32_jonah/jonah.pdf

Young's Analytical Concordance.